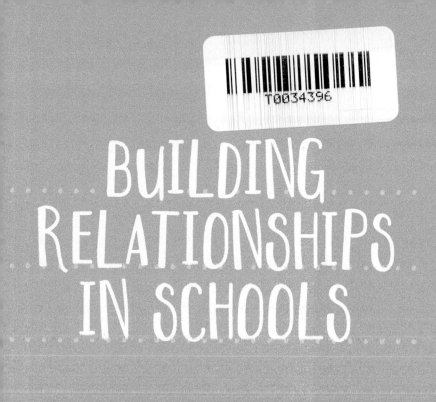

BUILDING
RELATIONSHIPS
IN SCHOOLS

BUILDING RELATIONSHIPS IN SCHOOLS

{  Omar Akbar }

1 Oliver's Yard
55 City Road
London EC1Y 1SP

CORWIN
A Sage company
2455 Teller Road
Thousand Oaks, California 91320
(800)233-9936
www.corwin.com

Unit No 323-333, Third Floor, F-Block
International Trade Tower, Nehru Place
New Delhi 110 019

8 Marina View Suite 43-053
Asia Square Tower 1
Singapore 018960

Editor: Delayna Spencer
Editorial assistant: Harry Dixon
Production editor: Rabia Barkatulla
Copyeditor: Bryan Campbell
Proofreader: Brian McDowell
Indexer: Michael Allerton
Marketing manager: Dilhara Attygalle
Cover design: Wendy Scott
Typeset by: C&M Digitals (P) Ltd, Chennai, India
Printed in the UK

**Library of Congress Control Number:
2023946078**

**British Library Cataloguing in
Publication data**

A catalogue record for this book is
available from the British Library

ISBN 978-1-5296-7286-2 (pbk)

This book Is dedicated to every teacher who wants to be remembered

TABLE OF CONTENTS

{ ABOUT THIS BOOK }

Relationship building is often described as being key to a teacher's success in and outside the classroom, but rarely is its nuanced nature analysed or practical advice ever given on how to get the best from working relationships. This book covers everything you need to know about relationship building with students, support staff, stakeholders and parents.

The Little Guide for Teachers series is little in size but BIG on all the support and inspiration you need to navigate your day to day life as a teacher.

- Authored by experts in the field
- Easy to dip in-and-out of
- Interactive activities encourage you to write into the book and make it your own
- Fun engaging illustrations throughout
- Read in an afternoon or take as long as you like with it!

Find out more at
www.sagepub.co.uk/littleguides

{ ABOUT THE SERIES }

THE LITTLE GUIDE FOR TEACHERS series is little in size but BIG on all the support and inspiration you need to navigate your day-to-day life as a teacher.

 IDEAS FOR THE CLASSROOM

HINTS & TIPS

REFLECTION

NOTE IT DOWN

www.sagepub.co.uk/littleguides

ABOUT THE AUTHOR

Omar Akbar is a secondary science teacher of 18 years in Birmingham and author of the bestselling trainee/ECT guide *The (Un)official Teacher's Manual: What they don't teach you in training* as well as *Bad School Leadership (and what to do about it)* and *Teaching for Realists: Making the Education System Work for You and Your Pupils*.

You can read Omar's blog at theunofficialteachersmanual.blog and follow him on: Twitter @UnofficialOA, Instagram: theunofficialteachersmanual, Facebook: The Unofficial Teacher's Manual. Omar also hosts *The Unofficial Teacher's Manual* podcast which is available on Spotify.

 @UNOFFICIALOA

THEUNOFFICIALTEACHERSMANUAL

THE UNOFFICIAL TEACHER'S MANUAL

INTRODUCTION

Relationships.

Anyone who has ever worked in a school will scream of their importance from the rooftops.

We take pride in a good relationship; we thrive, the kids thrive.

Bad relationships hinder and irritate; we struggle, the kids struggle.

The importance of relationships in a school setting is often discussed but rarely is solid advice ever given on how best to build positive relationships. While teachers successful in this area are recognised and praised, the nuance of their practice is seldom shared and, often, the good relationship is perceived to be a product of some elusive quality possessed by the individual. And this isn't without some merit: not everything is quantifiable – some people are just better at it than others.

If we look closely, however, we can see that there absolutely are things we can do (and not do!) to build positive relationships: relationship building is an art form in its own right and much of our success (or failure) is down to our own actions.

Thriving teachers build relationships in subtle and not-so-subtle ways, consciously and unconsciously employing very specific techniques.

We all know the firm but fun teachers who the kids like and respect in equal measure. We all know the teacher who seems to get their voice heard by SLT over others. We all know teachers that other teachers just seem to gravitate more towards. So, what is it exactly that they do?

In a school setting, relationships are indeed of paramount importance – a make or break. In this book we explore how best to develop the six types of relationship that a teacher has, namely:

- With an entire class

- With individual pupils

- With fellow teachers

- With school leaders

- With support staff

- With parents/carers

While the nature of individual relationships varies – your relationship with a pupil will never resemble your relationship with SLT! – there are four intertwined aims for every kind of teacher relationship:

- To ensure your own wellbeing

- To aid your professionalism/progression

- To increase your overall job satisfaction

- To maximise your pupils' outcomes

Rarely is one relationship entirely separable from another: e.g. your relationship with your SLT will likely be better if your relationship with your class is positive and your relationship with a class will likely be better if your relationship with individual pupils is positive. Make sense? So, while the advice in individual chapters can be taken in isolation, a holistic approach will help better achieve the aims of all school relationships.

So get your highlighters ready and learn how best to maximise your teaching potential in all areas!

CHAPTER 1

HOW TO BUILD A RELATIONSHIP WITH AN ENTIRE CLASS

In this chapter we explore:

- There is no such thing as perfection with regard to pupil achievement, behaviour, etc.; however, pupils do better overall when the teacher-class relationship is positive.
- A teacher should not lower their standards for the fear of being disliked by their class.
- A teacher can develop the teacher-class relationship by: being authentic, being passionate, being approachable, having a good sense of humour; by story-telling, making the curriculum relevant and being tactful when setting sanctions.

Before we begin, let's clarify something.

For all intents and purposes, there is no such thing as the 'perfect' classroom: You will never get pin drop silence for a full hour. You will never get a hundred per cent homework turnover. You will never get every child to engage with every topic, and every student will not thank you at the end of every lesson nor will they offer you an apple at the beginning. This bears no resemblance to school reality whatsoever.

In non-fictitious classrooms, some pupils will be less engaged than others. Some pupils will talk when you're talking. Some pupils will be defiant. Some pupils will hate the subject. Some pupils will hate all subjects. Some pupils will never appreciate your efforts. This is all perfectly 'normal'.

A good teacher-class relationship does not set out to seek 'perfection'. Rather, the children in your care do 'better' when your relationship with them is better: i.e. in a class where a positive teacher-class relationship is present, students are more likely to show good behaviour, be more enthused by the subject, work harder and generally be happier in the teacher's presence.

 ## REFLECTION POINTS

- **Think about a teacher from your school days that you and your classmates liked and respected. What qualities/characteristics did they have? Write in the space below.**

- **Think about a teacher from your school days that you and your classmates neither liked nor respected. What qualities/characteristics did they have?**

- **Use these reflections to consider how you will best develop your relationship with your class(es).**

HOW IS A GOOD TEACHER-CLASS RELATIONSHIP ACHIEVED?

It is worth noting here that we cannot – and must not if we care about teacher recruitment and retention at least – blame teachers for pupils' actions. What follows is not a silver-bullet as school culture, societal expectations and a myriad of other factors influence a child's relationship with education.

There is, nonetheless, a lot we can do as teachers. Take heed:

A HEALTH WARNING

Aim neither to be liked nor disliked. One would think the latter would be obvious, but some in the profession consider being disliked a strength because they believe it's proof of their strictness. This simply is not true and by the same token, whether they admit it or not, kids can tell the difference between what is good for them, i.e. rules, boundaries, etc. and what they 'like', i.e. uncontrolled social media use, TV, [insert as appropriate]. One only has to observe a class that has had a series of supply teachers for a half-term to see how frustrated pupils become with the lack of enforced boundaries and proper education that inevitably result from inconsistency. *In short, do not lower your standards in fear of being disliked as it leads to a poor teacher-class relationship in the long run.* The teacher who lets the pupils have their phones out whilst working because they want to appear 'cool' or 'safe' often ends up being disliked for their lack of effort and concern.

BE AN EXCELLENT TEACHER

A common trait of all teachers that have a good teacher-class relationship is that they are … wait for it … excellent teachers. Dear teachers, the basics matter. A lot. Get your planning, teaching, assessing and discipline en pointe and a good teacher-class relationship is likely to follow. Before you think to yourself, 'I can't possibly be excellent in every area!' It's fine – no one is. Just makes sure it's the bread and butter of teaching that you are excellent in: more often than not, it's what goes on in your classroom that makes you excellent in the eyes of your pupils (pun intended). Don't ignore everything else but do focus on that. Good lessons will lead to good pupil outcomes and therefore a better teacher-class relationship. In addition, by teaching good lessons, your pupils receive the message (albeit unconsciously) that you care. Again, such a perception is invaluable for a positive teacher-class relationship. Try going above and beyond here and there, perhaps? Don't worry – there is no need to increase your overall workload; something as simple as marking a test ready for the next lesson 'because I couldn't wait to see how well you all did!' is sufficient. And please, for the love of God, do not fall for this myth that teaching is a thankless profession. Granted, a pupil outright thanking you is something of a rare – or at least an end of year – occurrence but be sure that when a kid greets you in the corridor or a group of kids come to see you at break for some seemingly inane reason, for example, what they are actually doing is thanking you.

TELL A STORY

A teacher-class relationship can be nurtured by increasing pupils' enthusiasm for the subject/topic. To do this, add a personal touch through story telling. For example, a biology teacher teaching DNA may want to talk about the results of an ancestry test they once took. A physics teacher may want to relate force, mass, and acceleration back to their university rugby playing days. There are countless examples. It doesn't have to be a crazy story with an unexpected punchline, but it does help if the story is personal to you in some way. You'd be surprised how quickly enthusiasm for a subject/topic increases once it's put into a liveable context. When telling a story, don't overreach and be sure not to overshare! There is no need to tell your students about the time you were drunk at university and stole a load of road signs on the way home from a night club you got kicked out of because you projectile-vomited all over the bartender. That's got nothing at all to do with photosynthesis and will probably get you called into a meeting or two. Keep it relevant and try not to go too far off topic lest you end up being a distraction for your pupils!

MAKE IT RELEVANT

In addition to telling a story, another way to increase enthusiasm is by making the subject/topic relevant to pupils' daily lives where possible. For example, a chemistry teacher may relate a given organic compound to the manufacture of medicinal drugs. A maths teacher may relate ratio calculations to cake baking. Again, there are countless examples and just like when telling a story, it is not necessary to 'entertain,' i.e. you don't have to give a 'wacky' or unique example. Basics are sufficient to get the desired effect. There is nothing, of course, stopping you from being wacky/unique but it is by no means necessary. Simply making an attempt to reach pupils at their level (by making it relevant and/or by telling a story) not only increases their enthusiasm but it raises your personability – both of which are key to a successful teacher-class relationship.

HINTS AND TIPS

When planning your lessons, have a mental box for relevance and note down how the subject area can be made relevant to daily life.

BE AUTHENTIC

The hallmark of a teacher with a good teacher-class relationship is their authenticity. Whilst it may be difficult to define, we can be certain of one thing: people – particularly kids – know authenticity when they see it/lack of it. Seemingly, it is an aura or vibe that people pick up on through a mix of our words, actions, and body language. Granted, we may alter the aforementioned characteristics on a situation-by-situation basis and of course that is perfectly normal, i.e. you don't have to speak to your pupils as you would your friends in order to appear authentic. There is no need to lose your teacher voice, posture, gesticulation, etc.; however, it is not unreasonable to suggest that those who genuinely believe in the importance of their job and have a genuine interest in the pupils they teach are probably more likely to be perceived as authentic because, oddly enough, they are authentic! The beliefs you carry will be depicted by your words, actions, and body language. Believe in teaching. Believe in the teacher – you.

BE PASSIONATE

Teachers with a good teacher-class relationship are often passionate about their subject/topics. Passion is contagious so pupils will naturally become more enthusiastic when in the presence of a passionate teacher and a good teacher-class relationship is likely to follow. Be overtly passionate not only about the subject/topic but also pupil achievement. Like authenticity, passion is also a vibe that people pick up on through a mix of our words, actions, and body language. With passion however, there is a little more wriggle room. Your tone likely changes when you talk about something you're passionate about – embrace this change in the classroom! If a kid does well in a test, shout about it. If you're fascinated by natural selection, make sure the whole class knows! If your passion is not obvious from your tone of voice (or indeed, even if it is) another way to show passion for your subject is to plaster your classroom walls with displays of whatever subject/topic you are passionate about. They may or may not have any learning value directly, but overt passion is contagious and ultimately improves the teacher-class relationship, improving pupil outcomes.

HAVE A SENSE OF HUMOUR

From my favourite French teacher, who once scrunched up a piece of paper and threw it at my friend's face, saying: 'Ha! I got you back!' (to be fair, he *did* throw paper at her the lesson before – although I don't advise you try this), to perhaps your nice but stern, dry-witted history teacher whose eye roll at a silly comment was enough to get the class chuckling, it seems a teacher's sense of humour – however blunt or subtle – goes hand-in-hand with a good teacher-class relationship. Humour obviously has entertainment value, but it is a strong indicator of emotional intelligence which is a key ingredient for *any* relationship. Of course, some people are funnier than others – no teacher is expected to be a stand-up comedian – but revealing your humorous side is always beneficial. Do be careful when being funny, however, as again, you don't want to be the one distracting your pupils. Make sure your boundaries are well established early on and that the class know exactly when you're 'being funny' and when you're 'being serious.' Develop your ability to make an effective and clear switch between the two.

BE APPROACHABLE

Contrary to popular belief, being approachable doesn't mean you have to reach Mary Poppins' level of friendliness: you don't have to constantly smile, enthusiastically greet every student that walks past you, or always display open body gestures. Yes, that is *one* way of appearing approachable (and it's a good way!) but what you need to do is be approachable in *your* way. If your teaching persona is a bit sterner than the one described, it's fine *as long as you are still approachable*. So, if greeting a pupil with a radiant smile is not in your repertoire, then by all means do it your way – which may just be an approving head-nod followed by a stern sounding 'good morning'. What's important is that it *is* done, not necessarily *how* it's done. Kids are savvy to differences in personality, i.e. they aren't expecting nor wanting the same from every teacher. Nonetheless, in essence, an approachable teacher is one who talks to their pupils *when they don't have to*, i.e. outside of simply just teaching them. Something seemingly trivial like meeting and greeting your class at the door will go a long way toward facilitating pupils' perception of you as an approachable teacher, thereby improving the teacher–class relationship. (More guidance of how, when, etc. to talk to pupils follows in the next chapter.)

GIVE SANCTIONS RELUCTANTLY

Behaviour policies will vary from school to school and you as a professional will decide how best to utilise school policy in a given situation. What you can be sure of, however, is that teachers with a good teacher–class relationship issue sanctions with a great deal of reluctance. 'Joe, you are giving me no other choice but to give you a detention. I've asked you politely three times,' will facilitate a good teacher-class relationship far more than: 'Right. That's it. Outside. NOW! I said NOW!' Don't beat yourself up over it: we all end up reacting rather than responding at some stage in our careers, but try your hardest not to portray yourself as 'trigger-happy' with sanctions as, ultimately, punishments – when issued wrongly or excessively – can erode the teacher–class relationship.

If you assert yourself in the correct way, it is possible to avoid poor behaviour – and therefore the need to sanction – altogether. Focus particularly on your teacher-voice. Avoid being monotonous at all costs and adopt specific tones for specific situations. For example, your tone for saying: 'Let's listen to the cells song!' to an enthusiastic year 7 class must be very different to your: 'Right. We need to keep it down now. Five minutes pin-drop silence while you complete the questions,' to a noisy year 9 class. Your change in tone should be distinct and apparent. Teachers with a good teacher–class relationship rely on *themselves* before relying on school systems, so as well as being mindful of your teacher-voice, also be mindful of your teacher-space: walk around the room whilst actually teaching – not just when checking work. If you have some low-level disruptors, simply standing next to them is often sufficient to get them to stop. By moving around the room, the message pupils get is that they are in *your* territory so *your* rules apply. And finally, be mindful of your body language: back straight and shoulders back. You have to appear confident, in control and unaffected emotionally by any poor behaviour. Regardless of how flustered you may feel because your laptop crashed this morning and your lesson's not as well planned as it could've been, it must not show on your face.

NOTE IT DOWN

COMPLETE THE TABLE TO MAKE A NOTE OF THE STORIES YOU MIGHT SHARE WITH YOUR CLASS(ES):

Subject/Topic	Story – key points
•	
•	
•	

CHAPTER 2
HOW TO BUILD A RELATIONSHIP WITH INDIVIDUAL PUPILS

In this chapter we explore:

- There is no such thing as perfection with regard to pupil achievement, behaviour, etc.; however, a child will likely do better overall if they have a positive relationship with the teacher.
- A good teacher-pupil relationship can have a lasting impact on a child's life chances.
- A teacher can build a good relationship with pupils by: chatting to their pupils, giving sincere praise, contacting parents, being tactful with sanctions, running an after-school club or organising a trip.

Much like the teacher–class relationship, the teacher–pupil relationship does not seek out 'perfection'. Rather, a pupil with whom a teacher has a positive relationship will display better behaviour, have more enthusiasm for the subject, work harder and generally be happier in the teacher's presence than they perhaps would otherwise. Better outcomes will likely follow.

A good teacher–pupil relationship can have a massive impact on a child's life chances; we don't need to look far to find proof: Olympic gold medalist Mohammed Farah credits his former PE teacher, Mr Watkinson, for spotting Mo's talent and nurturing his potential. Mr Watkinson was even best man at Farah's wedding! Arsenal legend Ian Wright held back his tears when he was reunited with his former teacher, Mr Pigden, whose support, Wright says, gave him direction and purpose as a troubled child.

The list is a long one. What a blessed profession to be in.

Of course, we will not have the level of impact of Mr Watkinson and Mr Pidgen on every child in our care. In fact, we may never have that level of impact on any child. One thing, however, is for certain:

You *will* have an impact. A significant one. A good one.

So how do we build a positive teacher–pupil relationship?

Before we begin, it is worth noting that the advice in the previous chapter can also apply on a one-to-one basis. Group dynamics of course are different to that of individual settings so different strategies take priority in the former, but ultimately, groups are composed of individuals so, in this case, being approachable, having a sense of humour, telling a story, etc., all work with individuals. In addition, a reminder that we must not blame adults for the actions of children and also, dear teachers, do not lower your standards for fear of being disliked.

TALK TO YOUR PUPILS

Common sense, right? But it isn't that simple. In the previous chapter we discussed the importance of approachability and the importance of talking to your pupils outside of what is necessary. But you've got a class to teach: you don't have time for chit-chat, right?

Or do you?

Hand-in-hand with approachability goes good communication. As a teacher, you have to decide how, when, where, and for how long you should talk to a pupil/s in order to build a good teacher–pupil relationship.

ENGAGE IN CHIT-CHAT

Once your expectations have been established, you can begin to chit-chat. Let's say, for example, you're almost at half-term in with your new class. They know your boundaries: when you're being serious, when you're being funny, when you're happy, when you're annoyed, etc. The class are largely compliant and there are no regular major misbehaviours. This is a good point (albeit not the only point) at which to develop the teacher-pupil relationship somewhat. Every so often, work your way around the room and talk to a pupil/s individually about something unrelated to your lesson. It could be football, music, a TV show, etc. The topic is not particularly important, nor do you have to show that you're 'down with kids' for this to have the desired effect. The *way* you talk, however, is important. Consider losing your teacher voice somewhat and adopt a more casual tone – not too much and of course be sensitive to the year group – but just enough to indicate that you are being friendly but not trying to be friends. If you are stuck for conversation, just listen to the kids murmur and chip in where you deem appropriate. The point is that you are showing your pupils that you are genuinely interested in them as people and are not just performing the function of a teacher. On this note, you'll be surprised how much your pupils are interested in *you*. By simply circulating the room, casually chatting here and there, pupils will ask you every question from, 'What football team do you support, Miss?' to the one that I once got: 'Sir, do bald men have to use shampoo?' Jokes aside, such questions/conversations are also good to facilitate a teacher-pupil relationship. Respond to pupils as long as you are comfortable doing so.

BE CONTROLLED

Be very controlled when engaging in chit-chat. Again, make sure your expectations have been established but also be mindful of time. If you let it get out of control, behaviour in the class is likely to dip as pupils will see you as a 'mate' rather than the authority in the room. Remember, be friendly but don't be friends. You will easily sense if the chit-chat is getting out of control at which point do not hesitate to revert to pin-drop silence 'until everyone's finished,' for example. The good thing, is that to build a good teacher-pupil relationship, a few minutes chit-chat every few lessons with small groups of pupils or an individual pupil is sufficient.

BREAK AND LUNCH

Break and lunchtime duty are a good time to chit-chat as you have fewer time constraints. It is not uncommon for groups of pupils to approach a teacher on duty for no other reason than a chit-chat so, when this happens, take advantage! It is ok to initiate chit-chat whilst on duty, but if you do, keep it brief: most kids do not want to spend their break time talking to a teacher. That aside, go all out in showing your human (but still professional) side.

 IDEAS FOR THE CLASSROOM

Choose a class in which you have well-established boundaries and expectations. Circulate the room whilst the class is working and chat to pupils about some unrelated topic for a few minutes. How did pupils respond? Were you able to maintain discipline during/after? What will you do the same/differently next time?

GIVE WARM, SINCERE PRAISE

Every school (rightly so) has a rewards system to complement their behaviour system. Teachers – again, rightly so – are encouraged to reward pupils for anything consistently positive in order that the child remains motivated and feels their accomplishments have been recognised. And that is all good. If you want to develop your relationship with individual pupils, however, you just need to add a bit of *warm, sincere praise* when issuing a reward. So for example, as we are very busy as teachers we may just robotically put a merit point on the board and say 'well done' to the student who performs the highest in the class on an assessment. Our relationship with the pupil would improve significantly if we just got the class quiet and said something to the effect of: 'That is some of the best work I've seen in a long time. If you keep this up, you'll be able to have any career you choose.' It's the words you say that the child will remember and recall years later – not the sticker: it's your words that will develop the teacher-pupil relationship. It goes without saying that warm, sincere praise is not reserved for 'high achievers' only. When given to a child who was previously struggling with xyz but has recently improved, you'd be surprised how much warm, sincere praise will keep them motivated and improve the teacher-pupil relationship.

PHONE HOME

Whether it's for a positive reason, e.g. to reward, or a negative reason, e.g. to report a behaviour concern, the impact of a five minute phone call on the teacher–pupil relationship cannot be underestimated. As mentioned in the previous chapter, much of what makes for a good relationship (any relationship) is dependent upon personability. By phoning home, again, you are showing your own personal involvement in a given situation, thereby making it clear to a pupil that you care and are not just carrying out the function of a teacher. Of course, Jimmy may temporarily hate you for 'grassing him up' to his parents, but be certain that if you later phone them again when Jimmy's behaviour has improved, he will be overjoyed. The same is true for Saira who is never late, always completes her homework, does well in every assessment, never has any behaviour issues etc. Saira will probably get a certificate at the end of the year but it would be better for you and her, i.e. the teacher-pupil relationship, if you rang home a couple of times before then. Make it part of your teaching repertoire to phone home for both rewards and sanctions.

⌐   HINTS AND TIPS

Make five positive phone calls home every two weeks. In a given
class, for example, ring the parents/carers of three pupils who
have shown consistently good effort, of one whose behaviour
has improved significantly, and of another who did exceptionally
well in the last assessment.

REQUEST A MEETING

At some point in your career, you may come across a pupil who has decided
(for any of many reasons/non-reasons) that they hate your guts and may
even be outright hostile in your presence. You will likely have sanctioned
them several times for their misbehaviour priorly but to no avail. In order
to rescue the teacher–pupil relationship, you have to act *before* it gets to
this stage. When you can see the relationship beginning to decline, request
a meeting with a pastoral lead and the child. What actually happens in the
meeting does not have to be 'scripted,' i.e. you don't need to ask them a
series of questions: 'What happened?' 'What were you thinking?' 'How did
you feel when . . .' etc. Just adopt a friendly tone and tell the child you don't
have any issue with them personally; you think they have a lot of potential
etc. Keep it positive but re-establish your expectations and display the same
reluctance to sanction-setting mentioned in the previous chapter.

RUN AN AFTER-SCHOOL CLUB OR GO ON A TRIP

If you have a hobby/interest out of work that can be tied in with work, then
doing so will do wonders for your relationship with your pupils. Teachers
that excel in these are more often than not perceived as a *person* rather
than a *function*. The majority of our classroom time is spent carrying out
our function (and should be, of course!) but that function can be better
performed if pupils see a different side to us. By showing pupils our personal
interests and teaching knowledge and skills in an environment that has
less conventional rules, expectations and boundaries than a classroom,
the teacher–pupil relationship improves because again, you are perceived
as more personable. Young people often have a binary rather than a fluid

perception of people – 'Mr Bloggs is serious,' 'Mr Johnson's a geek,' etc. Running a dance, boxing, origami, baking, [insert as appropriate] club for as little as thirty minutes a week may just be enough to alter that perception and allow your pupils to respond even better because now they know there's more to you than they first thought! A little health warning: if you decide to run an after-school club or something similar, do not do it to the detriment of your own wellbeing. As we are all constrained by time, it is perfectly acceptable to prioritise tasks and if running an after-school club is not possible for you, then, don't. What matters is *that* you prioritise relationship building not necessarily *how* you prioritise relationship building.

Being present on a school trip can have the same effect. If you can, get on to one! The only difference between a club and a trip is that on a trip you should be more vigilant (as you are in unfamiliar settings, accidents could have worse consequences, etc.) than you would be in a classroom with ten pupils. Nonetheless, it is very common not only for teachers to build long-lasting bonds with pupils on school trips, but also long-lasting memories of the fun times of their career.

REFLECTION POINTS

What hobbies/interests do you have that you can incorporate into your teaching? How could you go about doing this? An after school/lunch/break time club? What impact might it have on your relationship with your pupils?

NOTE IT DOWN

WHICH OF YOUR PUPILS DO YOU THINK WOULD BENEFIT FROM A MEETING?

WHY?

WHAT WILL YOU SAY IN THE MEETING?

HOW WILL YOU MEASURE ITS IMPACT?

AFTER THE MEETING:

WHAT WERE THE KEY TAKE-AWAYS FROM THE MEETING?

WHAT HAS BEEN THE IMPACT?

WHAT WILL YOU DO THE SAME/DIFFERENTLY NEXT TIME (IN A MEETING)?

CHAPTER 3
HOW TO BUILD A RELATIONSHIP WITH FELLOW TEACHERS

In this chapter we explore:

- As a teacher, your wellbeing, progression, and overall job satisfaction rely heavily on your relationship with fellow teachers.
- Teacher camaraderie is doubly important because anxiety and stress in the teaching profession are disproportionately high.
- To maintain good teacher–teacher relationships, don't be a busybody, a martyr, or a mood hoover. Instead, be supportive, offer praise, be personable, and balance positivity with authenticity.

It is no secret that schools are perpetually subjected to external pressures (namely the government and Ofsted) and that these lead to an increase in internal pressures and demands on school staff. It is because of this, sadly, that the teaching profession is one in which rates of anxiety and stress are disproportionately high.

Teacher camaraderie is therefore of utmost importance: *The teacher–teacher relationship is as important as the teacher–class and teacher–pupil relationship*. At some point in your career, you will need a shoulder to cry on, someone to rant to, someone's lesson plan, someone's interview notes, someone to drive you home, someone to … [insert as appropriate]. You need your colleagues and your colleagues need you. Your wellbeing, progression and overall job satisfaction depend greatly upon your relationship with fellow teachers so it is important for you to nourish this relationship like you would any other.

Having a good relationship with fellow teachers is a make-or-break deal: Teachers who believe *and live* the words: *we are in this together* do markedly better in the aforementioned areas than those who don't.

In order to be a supportive, well-liked, and well-respected teacher, there are things we should do and there are things that we shouldn't.

 ## REFLECTION POINTS

Think about a teacher who you consider to have a good relationship with fellow teachers. What qualities/characteristics do they possess?

Think about a teacher who you consider to have a poor relationship with fellow teachers. What qualities/characteristics do they possess?

Use these reflections to consider how best you will develop your relationship with fellow teachers.

TYPES OF BEHAVIOURS TO AVOID

In schools, it seems to be the case that the same traits are found universally annoying! Whatever you do, don't be a busybody, a martyr, or a mood hoover. (NB The descriptions that follow are for the sake of humour and ease only. Human personalities are too fluid to be placed in simple boxes, so it is better to look out for traits instead of labelling the whole person!)

THE BUSYBODY

The inability of some teachers to mind their own business grinds the gears of fellow teachers. The hallmark of a busybody is offering unsolicited advice condescendingly, in a way that suggests that they know more, hence undermining their colleagues. In addition, a busybody may comment negatively on the practice of another teacher or at least imply negativity by using education's most loathed phrase: 'Well, they behave for me!' for example, or something analogous depending on the situation. Busybodies make the assumption that because they do xyz in a particular way, their way is the only correct way and everyone else is wrong – and it is their duty to tell everyone they're wrong. Given the scrutiny that teachers are already under, the last thing any teacher wants is a fellow teacher commenting on their practice out of turn. If you *really* see someone doing something that you feel could be improved or avoided, simply say: 'I have a suggestion' then wait for a response. Otherwise, leave the managing to the school leaders.

THE MARTYR

You know that teacher who works mornings, evenings, break times, lunchtimes, weekends – just like the rest of us – *but won't shut up about it*? That's the martyr. Of course, no one should be working in the hyperbolic way described but what makes the martyr stand out is their holier than thou attitude, i.e. they imply that they are doing more work than you. 'Well, some of us don't have time to go the gym!' you'll hear them say when heaven forbid, someone says they're going to the gym after school. 'Well, if no one else is going to volunteer for it, I might as well volunteer *again*' – when no one wants to do another Saturday revision session.

With the average teacher working 50–55 hours a week, no one, rightly so, wants it said or implied that they are not doing enough. If you decide to go above and beyond, firstly you will probably burn out more quickly and secondly, rubbing it in people's faces will make you unpopular. Be humble.

THE MOOD HOOVER

There is nothing wrong with (and I would argue that it's probably therapeutic) for teachers to have a good old moan. Grumbling, griping, sounding off and kicking off are all part and parcel of being a teacher... in the right time, frequency, and place.

The mood hoover, however, is not simply a stressed/tired teacher letting off steam. The mood hoover is a teacher who is negative All. The. Time. Negative about anything and everything. It could be the smallest initiative from SLT and they will look long and hard to find reasons why it's a bad idea; they'll have problems for every solution. They will rant at you in the corridor, at the photocopier, and in the car park about some inane thing that you wouldn't have given two s***s about had you not had the misfortune of bumping into them.

Negativity breeds negativity and it is easy to descend into a downward spiral. A teacher will inevitably go through periods of stress, feeling undervalued, etc. and that is normal (rightly or wrongly) in our profession. The problem is that a mood hoover will make you feel even worse during these times by adding to your woes with ten of theirs – that's the last thing any teacher needs. Instead of a mood hoover then, be someone who *sympathises* with a teacher who may feel stressed, tired, anxious etc. but do not indulge them. Have a: 'It'll be over soon' or 'It won't matter next week' or 'You'll get through it' kind of attitude without dismissing their concerns completely.

It is also worth noting that mood hoovers are more often than not known by SLT as, inevitably, word gets round. Their chances of promotion become limited, and they may find themselves being 'learning-walked' more often than other teachers. In all honesty, would you want your kids taught by a mood hoover?

So what can we do instead to foster good working relationships with fellow teachers?

BE PROFESSIONALLY SUPPORTIVE

Teaching is made easier when teachers help other teachers. Working with supportive colleagues not only aids the development of our practice, but also does wonders for our wellbeing. Naturally, the teacher–teacher relationship improves. How, exactly does one provide support for fellow teachers? First off, share your resources. Most schools have some sort of system whereby you can easily access departmental resources, for example, but it is still normal for certain topics/subjects to be incomplete, missing, in need of updating, etc. If you're aware of a teacher planning a lesson from scratch on a topic you've taught three times before, simply saying: 'I've got a Power Point and a worksheet on that. Just email me if you want it,' will go a long way to facilitate the relationship between you and the recipient. By the same token, if you can see a teacher is struggling with a system, e.g. report writing, data entry, rewards, sanctions etc., then offer your help. This one is particularly important when dealing with new teachers, as often they fear they'll come across as pesky if they keep asking questions. If you're an experienced member of staff, check up on them.

'BIG UP' YOUR COLLEAGUES

You'd be surprised how big the impact of something so small can be.

If you hear something good about another teacher, go out of your way to tell them. Let's say you overhear two kids talking about how much they enjoy Miss Khan's lessons. A two-line email to Miss Khan could be the one thing she needed to lift her mood after a long, tiring week. She will arrive at her next lesson with more confidence, feeling good about her job and ultimately her pupils will also benefit. Teachers with good teacher–teacher relationships often do so because they share other teachers' strengths and make them realise their potential. It is not necessary to send emails every week of course – overdoing it comes across as pretentious anyway – and sometimes just validating another teacher's expertise is enough: 'I walked past your room the other day when you had year 10. What were you doing? They looked really engrossed!' In short, be a teacher who acts as a buffer against external stressors: for every government minister that tells us we're not good enough, or not doing enough, there should be a colleague who tells us we are.

DON'T FORGET THE BASICS

Try not to forget the basics. It can be difficult for a busy teacher but do try to get it right most of the time. Smile. Greet anyone you walk past. Make small talk where possible. Listen. Empathise. Show good humour. Help create a positive whole school atmosphere by talking to those outside of your department. As in the previous section, small gestures can go a long way. In addition to the obvious reasons to be mindful of the basics, much of how well your ideas are going to be received by others will be decided by how well others respond to you *as a person*. Granted, it is not always the case, but you are in a far better position to achieve *and sustain* a promotion if fellow teachers already warm to you. Of course, the basics come more easily to some people than others: you may be shy, less socially confident, introverted or just less inclined to small talk. It's not a problem because in no workplace are personalities monolithic. If you struggle in some areas, just do more in other areas to maintain good teacher–teacher relationships.

HINTS AND TIPS

Bring cakes, biscuits etc. to the staffroom for 'no reason' (if you can). Being associated with anything sweet will do wonders for your relationship with your colleagues!

BALANCE POSITIVITY WITH AUTHENTICITY

Teaching is quite obviously a job which requires a positive mindset. A positive outlook is better for kids, and colleagues generally respond better to a glass-half-full person. There is, however, a type of positivity through which you risk making yourself unpopular with fellow teachers.

To put it bluntly – *teachers who are positive all the time about anything and everything are disingenuous.* Again, to be direct, there are things that a teacher has to do which are long-winded, time consuming or unnecessary – or at least perceived as such – and therefore not really possible to be enthusiastic about. You will never hear a teacher say: 'I really can't wait to enter the results of the mock exams, question by question. It'll be the best 90 minutes of my life!' The hyper-positive teacher then, is usually just someone who wants their next promotion; a careerist who probably cares more about 'status' than they do about the kids. (There are other, less polite ways of describing this teacher, but we'll refrain from those for now).

Teachers with good teacher–teacher relationships balance their positivity with authenticity. In other words, they are not afraid to acknowledge that the job can get the better of them too sometimes, but they nonetheless maintain a positive frame. They join in the staffroom rants as and when appropriate and if some new initiative is going to make no difference to pupil outcomes whatsoever, they *will* mention it to fellow teachers and not just pretend it's the best thing since sliced bread. Granted, the balance between positivity and authenticity is a fine one (to be elaborated upon in the next chapter) but, for now, remember that the teacher–teacher relationship is founded on a shared experience. If you set yourself apart by being unrealistically positive, fellow teachers will not see you as one of them and you might end up losing the support that you may one day need.

NOTE IT DOWN

Make a note of what you could do to build positive relationships with colleagues.

Here are a few examples to get you started:

- Send a positive email to a new teacher; ensure their line manager is cc'd in.

- Comment positively on a colleague's teaching one lunchtime.

- Go out of your way to share resources.

- Initiate small talk with someone you don't normally chat with.

CHAPTER 4
HOW TO BUILD A RELATIONSHIP WITH SCHOOL LEADERS

In this chapter we explore:

- For a school to function effectively, teachers and school leaders must show empathy towards each other's roles.
- The aim of the teacher–leader relationship is to ensure that you, as the teacher, stand out as a good practitioner and as someone who recognises the importance of teamwork.
- To maintain a good relationship with school leaders: don't go above their head, don't add to their workload unnecessarily; be yourself (but not too much!), push their ethos, don't disagree disagreeably, and be authentic but savvy.

As a general rule, teacher relationships are less 'familiar', so to speak, the further you go up the hierarchy. A headteacher, for example, will more often than not maintain a solely professional relationship with a teacher. A teacher's relationship with their immediate line manager, however, will likely be closer, and the most 'familiar' relationships are between fellow teachers. As there is an imbalance of power in the former, they cannot have the same dynamics as the latter. So naturally, those relationships cannot be built in the same dynamic as was with fellow teachers.

Your relationship with school leaders is two-fold and two-way. As well as the aims outlined in the introduction, the purpose of the relationship is not only for you to ensure that you stand out as a good teacher, but also as someone who is aware that in order for any school to function at its best, teachers and school leaders have to show empathy towards each other's roles: teaching a full timetable day in, day out, is bloody hard. Being accountable to Ofsted, parents and governors is bloody hard. Both parties must work together.

In this spirit then, here are some do's and don'ts for the teacher–leader relationship.

 REFLECTIONS

If you were a school leader/line manager, what three qualities would you want from the teachers you are responsible for?

Use your answers to consider how best you can display these qualities.

DON'T GO ABOVE THEIR HEAD

Keep things as in-house as you can. If you ever have an issue with a middle leader, don't go blabbing it to a senior leader. It is often said that the toughest place to be in a school is in the middle, so it is inevitable that not every head of department/subject/key stage, etc. is going to have done everything perfectly. The schemes of work may not be finished; they may not get round to sending you the document they said they would, and the meeting with Joe Bloggs' parents may not end up happening. Cover – don't advertise – their mishaps and if you have any issues, go to them directly wherever possible as first port of call. It is worth noting here that it will not necessarily be the case that a senior leader will come down on a middle leader like a tonne of bricks when given news of a mistake. But why pass it on? You'd be pretty annoyed if someone went and told your line manager how crap your last lesson with year 9 was, surely? Instead, have that extra bit of sympathy to keep the teacher–leadership relationship intact. Throwing someone under the bus is never a good look.

DON'T ADD TO THEIR WORKLOAD

If you think you get a lot of emails every day, why don't you take a look at the inbox of a school leader. It really is non-stop. From the inane to the important, school leaders are bombarded with emails throughout the day. Obviously, if you need to contact a school leader, you need to contact a school leader – that goes without saying – but the key word here is 'need'. There is a difference between having a genuine concern/request and going to a school leader for something the teacher in the class next door can tell you. As a general rule, a question about anything procedural or relating to school systems, e.g. data entry, rewards, sanctions, etc., does not require explaining by a school leader as pretty much anyone who has done it before can tell you. Always ask yourself: *Is this the only person who can help?*

By the same token, if you see a school leader struggling with a task and you are able to assist, then offer to lend a hand even if the task doesn't fall within your remit. Let's say, for example, that your head of department hasn't finished their bit of scheme work yet and you, having already finished yours, know you could quite easily finish theirs - offer to help.

Again, the little things will not go unnoticed. By not adding to a school leader's workload, you are giving them the message that you are both independent and considerate. By offering your help you are showing again that not only are you considerate but also that you are a dedicated professional.

BE YOURSELF... BUT NOT TOO MUCH

Relax. There's nothing wrong with you. Even if there was, school leaders will see you every day so any front you try and put on probably won't last. Luckily, no one's asking that of you! It is a good idea, however, to be a little less liberal with the version of yourself that you portray to school leaders. For example, you may have no qualms about telling your teacher-bestie that you haven't marked a year 8 book all half-term or that your Monday morning lessons weren't planned properly because you had a two-day hangover from Friday. The problem(?), however, is that as no one is with a teacher all the time in the classroom, school leaders base their judgements on how you come across, what your pupils say, what colleagues say, etc. So, for the sake of your own reputation, be a bit more reserved around a school leader lest they get the wrong impression. Don't get paranoid of course – they know you are human too and are more than likely a reasonable person – just be that little bit more mindful.

Off the back of this, remember that familiarity and friendship are not synonymous: don't assume that because your line manager, for example, is friendly, socialises with their team, etc. that they will be 'relaxed' in other areas. Like you, they too have a job to do so be assured that if you go opening your big mouth about those year 8 books you still haven't looked at, you risk getting hit with a book scrutiny by the very person you thought was 'laid back!' Again, just be that little bit more mindful.

HINTS AND TIPS

When speaking to senior leaders, be 'smart casual'. There is no need to be ultra formal but don't be overly friendly/ familiar either. Remember, judgements can be made on how you come across, so be mindful of unwittingly coming across as less professional than you may well be! When you're a well-established, good teacher however, you can relax a bit more.

PUSH THEIR ETHOS

You don't have to go around quoting the school motto, mission statement or whatever to every teacher you pass in the corridor, but school leaders need to know that you buy into whatever their focus, idea, or ethos might be. A large amount of what they do relies on school 'culture,' i.e. group behaviour, and group behaviour is ultimately the collective actions of individuals. What a school leader needs to be sure of is that you are someone who aids – not obstructs – their ideas. For example, let's say your school or even just your department has a new marking policy. Like with any other school policy, criticising it is easy. Instead of finding fault with it, why not talk to your colleagues about how it's saving you lots of time, or the kids are finding it more helpful than the previous one. This is not the unnecessary and effusive positivity described in the previous chapter, rather, it is simply providing support to school leaders. Remember – for a school to function, support has to be two-way. Having the aura of a teacher who is on board will do wonders for the teacher–leader relationship. (Of course, you are not expected to agree with every single initiative ever and are perfectly entitled to voice your concerns in the correct manner. If you are on board with something, however, show that you are!)

MOAN TACTFULLY

As explained in the previous chapter, moaning and ranting are inevitable and, in my opinion, part of a teacher's unwritten job description! Be mindful, however, of who you're moaning in front of. You will likely not have as much contact with school leaders as you will with fellow teachers, so if in the times that they do see you you're moaning or complaining about something seemingly minor, you risk their having a perception of you that you may deem unfair: Rightly or wrongly, school leaders will extrapolate: i.e. if you're always ranting and complaining, they may assume that you don't like being a teacher and therefore are probably not doing your best for your pupils. Be authentic but be savvy: save the moaning for fellow teachers lest you end up with more learning walks than you'd like!

As well as your general perception, consider also your career progression: whether or not you'll get promoted is ultimately decided by a school leader. If progression is what you want, school leaders have to be confident that you are someone who will take things in stride and not be at odds with every idea put forward; being a school leader is difficult enough, so why would they appoint someone who is difficult to work with. Displaying a 'can-do' attitude will bring you far more success than a 'fault-finding' one. Be aware also that a middle leader's job is made more difficult by the fact that they often have to carry out initiatives that they themselves don't necessarily agree with – such is the nature of the beast. The last thing they want is you doing their head in on top of that, so be mindful of this and don't be quick to pass judgement – inwardly or outwardly. It's just a job at the end of the day, right?

WHEN DISAGREEING, DON'T BE DISAGREEABLE

If an initiative is introduced which you either cannot see the value in or the hours to impact ratio is unjustifiable in your mind, *and you are a well-established, good teacher,* then there is no harm in bringing your concerns to a school leader. You just have to go about it in the right way. (More on that later). What you should never do is have a prolonged, public argument with a school leader in a meeting, for example, in the presence of the rest of the team. It'll make the meeting more exciting for everyone watching, of course, but it will damage the teacher–leader relationship even if in your mind it's just a healthy debate. You will appear combative whether you like it or not, and it's not fair to the school leader, who – like you – is under constant pressure. Moreover, it won't give you the desired outcome anyway. Putting someone on the spot, arguing back and forth just makes them defensive. It is perfectly reasonable to have a question, e.g. How does this benefit the pupils? but accept whatever answer is given even if you don't agree.

So how does one disagree without being disagreeable? As it is very much situation specific, it really does depend. Generally speaking, it is better to involve only the necessary people at the first stage, i.e., if you're dying to express your opinion on the new marking policy then instead of kicking off in a meeting, make an appointment with the relevant school leader and bend their ear back for fifteen minutes. Having said that, changes are never made off the back of the opinion of one teacher alone, so it doesn't really matter how much you protest solo. If you feel strongly, see what the feeling around school/your department is, then speak to a union rep who will make a judgement and contact the school leader concerned if necessary.

What is better than both disrupting a meeting and contacting a union rep is transparency. Do what is in your power to develop your teacher–leader relationship to the point that you can express any concerns you may have openly before you reach breaking point. Of course, this requires effort from both parties (school leaders should always be mindful of teacher wellbeing and workload) but you can put yourself in a better position to influence by being an excellent, authentic-but-savvy teacher.

NOTE IT DOWN

WHAT ARE YOUR SCHOOL'S/DEPARTMENT'S TARGETS AND/OR ETHOS?

HOW CAN YOU HELP INFLUENCE SCHOOL CULTURE IN ORDER TO PUSH THIS ETHOS/MEET THESE TARGETS?

CHAPTER 5

HOW TO BUILD A RELATIONSHIP WITH TEACHING ASSISTANTS (AND OTHER SUPPORT STAFF)

In this chapter we explore:

- The teacher–TA relationship is particularly important as it impacts pupils directly.
- A good teacher–TA relationship will therefore help to maximise pupil outcomes.
- You can build a positive teacher–TA relationship by: acknowledging your TA's expertise, sharing information with them effectively; by asking (not telling!) and by being mindful of your TA's workload and wellbeing.

Your relationship with your TA is of paramount importance as not only does it impact your daily practice in real time, but it also directly impacts the pupils for whom the TA may be responsible – often vulnerable pupils/pupils with very specific needs. You can get away with having a not-so-cordial relationship with a fellow teacher and your head of department may eventually forgive you for throwing them under the bus, but if there is animosity between you and your TA, be certain that your pupils will suffer.

It's not *all* down to the teacher, of course (every relationship is two-way) but there is a lot you can do to ensure a good working relationship with your TA, thereby maximising pupil outcomes.

Here's how to build the teacher–TA relationship.

 REFLECTION

How do you think your pupils could benefit from a positive teacher–TA relationship?

What expertise do you think a TA brings to the classroom?

Now think about how best you can create opportunities for the TA to utilise their expertise.

ACKNOWLEDGE THEIR EXPERTISE

You are the teacher, fully qualified and able to educate and improve the life chances of the children in your care – no one is debating that – but classroom-based support staff have very probably worked with considerably more pupils on a one-to-one basis than we have as teachers. For this reason, it is essential that we acknowledge their experience and their unique expertise. No teacher worth their salt would think otherwise, but it is still worth noting that TAs deserve the same level of professional respect that we do as teachers. While it is said and genuinely believed, it is not always shown. The way to show professional respect to a TA is by asking directly for advice, feedback and guidance on *your* practice wherever possible. If you have a TA for example, who assists a child with a high level of needs in your lesson, ask specifically if your strategies, resources etc. are working and what you can do to improve. This is not, of course, for the sole purpose of validating the TA's expertise, rather, it makes pragmatic sense as well because the pupils will ultimately benefit.

Another way to acknowledge the expertise of TAs is to be very specific with the tasks that you delegate and make sure they are child-centred, more often than not. The role of a TA may vary from key stage to key stage, but always bear in mind that it is not their job to make up for the bits that you accidentally omitted or just didn't pay enough attention to. A TA with whom you have a good relationship will save your life when it needs saving of course, but don't let this be the default position. Think carefully and specifically about what you want them to do.

HINTS AND TIPS

Have a quick chat with your TA at the end of every lesson. Ask for specific feedback – what went well, what could be improved, etc. This will acknowledge the TA's expertise as well as improve your practice.

SHARE INFORMATION EFFECTIVELY

TAs are as passionate about their job as teachers are and want to do it to the best of their ability. In order for the TA to have time to prepare, it is essential that all important information is shared well in advance: e.g., if there is a test coming up and Sarah needs a reader, email your TA the week before. If the seating plan is about to change, again, let your TA know beforehand. By promptly sharing information, not only will your TA have more time to prepare, but they will feel more valued as you're making it clear that their job is not just an add-on or an after-thought but something you value and acknowledge the impact of. Naturally, the teacher–TA relationship improves. Of course, it goes without saying that your pupils too will benefit from effective communication.

ASK, DON'T TELL

When making requests, always ask, never tell. There must be no indication from your tone that you perceive yourself to be higher up the hierarchy. Use phrases such as: 'Would you be able to …' or 'When you've got a moment, could you …' You're probably a decent person who would use these or something similar anyway, but it is still worth being reminded of as sometimes stress and time constraints can get the better of us. For the sake of the teacher–TA relationship, make this a priority. A TA who knows they're valued is more likely to go out of their way for you (and therefore the pupils) if ever needed. If you didn't get a chance to finish your marking, for example, they are more likely to offer help. If you didn't quite finish organising that school trip because you were busy designing the new scheme work, they may book the coach for you. Neither you nor the kids want to lose out on this support – which doesn't actually require that much from you to obtain!

BE MINDFUL OF THEIR WORKLOAD AND WELLBEING

Because the discussion on workload is often focused on teachers' workload alone, it is easy to forget that much of what applies to us applies to TAs: TAs also have more work than can be completed during contracted hours; TAs are also not paid sufficiently for the hours they put in; TAs are also highly accountable. Do not add to this if you can avoid it, lest the teacher–TA relationship suffers. Where possible, make a conscious effort to avoid last minute requests, short deadlines, or anything else you wouldn't respond particularly well to as a teacher. As mentioned earlier, your TA is far more likely to carry water for you (forgive the hyperbole) if they know you are mindful of their workload and wellbeing.

On a side note, it is worth noting that the teacher–TA relationship is one that your pupils will be able to observe first-hand. Use this as an opportunity to model good communication (or even a professional friendship) by *consciously remembering* to do everything you ask of your pupils, i.e. smile, make eye-contact, say please, thank you and show overt respect for your TA's professionalism.

REFLECTIONS

State three things you could learn from your TA in order to improve your practice.

SITE STAFF, IT STAFF, TECHNICIANS AND OFFICE STAFF (NON-CLASSROOM-BASED SUPPORT STAFF)

You will have significantly less daily contact with non-classroom-based support staff and your relationship with them will not directly impact your pupils, but nonetheless, all support staff are important to the effective running of a school. Here is some generic advice on how best to keep the teacher–support staff relationship positive.

KNOW THEIR NAMES

Craig will not give you the best laptop if you keep calling him Chris; Sharon won't bother getting your tax code changed so that you're not being emergency taxed if you keep confusing her with Lisa. Hyperbole aside, just like all other staff in a school, non-classroom-based support staff need to know that their contribution is valued and that they are seen as a person and not just a function. You may not deal with non-classroom-based support staff directly on a daily basis but learning their names does wonders for the teacher–support staff relationship. (Don't be surprised if Craig gives you a new laptop despite telling the teacher that keeps calling him Chris that there are no new ones!)

DON'T FORGET THE BASICS

Just like with fellow teachers, try not to forget the basics. It can be difficult for a busy teacher but do try to get it right most of the time. Smile. Greet anyone you walk past. Make small talk where possible. Listen. Empathise. Show good humour, etc. We are all part of the same professional family and small gestures can go a long way. A member of site staff once changed a flat tyre for an ECT. My guess is that he wouldn't have gone out of his way for someone with whom he didn't have a good rapport.

DON'T MAKE DEMANDS

Never allow your frustration to get the better of you: non-classroom-based support staff also have to prioritise and being p****d off is not enough to get you to the front of the queue – unfortunately. If the paper waste in your room has gotten out of hand, email Kevin and wait. If your laptop keeps crashing, log it with the helpdesk and wait for Craig to stop by instead of banging on his door in a frenzy. It probably won't work anyway (pun intended) but in any case, would you prioritise someone who thinks they're more important than everyone else?

SHOW THEM THAT THEY'RE VALUED

Sharon loves a box of chocolates on the last week of the winter term and Craig and his team are partial to a tin of biscuits or two. If you're ever being celebratory, e.g. your birthday, Christmas, Eid, end of term, end of year etc. always include (at least your immediate) non-classroom-based support staff. Just like TAs, non-classroom-based support staff often go beyond their contracted hours to get the job done. Show them they're valued.

FOLLOW PROCEDURE

If Imran says you need to give a week's notice for practical experiments, then guess what? You'd better give a week's notice if you want to make volcanoes with your year 7s like you promised them. If Kevin says you have to vacate the building by 6.30pm, then expect him to tell the Head when you leave at 6.46pm for the third day running. Dear teachers, procedure matters. What gives you the right to make Imran rush around for you or Kevin to stay behind to lock up when he should be at home. Support staff wellbeing matters as much as teacher wellbeing. Non-classroom-based support staff may be a step removed from the classroom, but we still need to make a conscious effort to be mindful.

GROVEL

Of course, you're a lovely person and would not deliberately skirt the guidelines in this section.

It is inevitable, however, that you will do something or other to p-off non-classroom-based support staff accidentally. You'll request a science practical that Imran spent forty-five minutes preparing, only to cancel it. You'll send a copy of the wrong exam paper to reprographics for it to be photocopied 500 times, and Sharon will probably get fed up with you not updating your personal details on the school system despite several requests.

When that happens, acknowledge your mistake and apologise. Better still, grovel. We're all busy and everyone makes mistakes, but again, don't let the fact that your job is somewhat removed from that of non-classroom-based support staff make you forget that their wellbeing and workload matter too. An apology will get you back in the good books and the teacher–support staff relationship will remain intact.

INVOLVE THEM IN THE DECISION-MAKING PROCESS

Imran will tell you point-blank that there's no way eight science teachers can do a heart dissection on the same day because it's impossible for him to get so many hearts from the butcher's so quickly. Kevin knows full well the chaos that will be caused if parents are allowed to park on lower school playground during parents' evening and Craig knows you'll probably be waiting twenty minutes if you just randomly show up to have your picture taken for your new lanyard. Where possible, try not to make a decision without involving non-classroom-based support staff, particularly where such a decision would impact them directly. Granted, major decisions are commonly made by school leaders, but as a classroom teacher nonetheless, it pays to be mindful where you can. So, if you've planned a dissection, check with Imran just to be sure. If you need to get your photo taken for a new lanyard, email Craig and ask him when it's best to stop by.

NOTE IT DOWN

DESCRIBE THREE THINGS THAT YOU WILL DO (OR DO MORE OF) TO DEVELOP YOUR RELATIONSHIP WITH YOUR TA.

HOW DO YOU THINK YOUR PUPILS WILL BENEFIT FROM EACH ONE?

Actions	Impact on Pupils

CHAPTER 6
HOW TO BUILD A RELATIONSHIP WITH PARENTS/CARERS

In this chapter we explore:

- Children tend to do better, attend, and enjoy school more when schools work together with families to support learning.
- The teacher–parent relationship will be more/less developed depending on the setting, i.e. primary teachers tend to have more frequent parental contact than secondary teachers. Choose/adapt the strategies in this chapter for your setting.
- As a teacher, you can develop a positive relationship with parents/carers, firstly by getting over your fear of them, and also by making positive phone calls home, by being honest, by knowing your pupils well, by sharing information promptly, by sharing your strategies and by being available.

A strong relationship between school and home is important as children tend to do better, attend and enjoy school more when schools work together with families to support learning. The teacher–parent relationship is therefore crucial to improving a child's life chances.

It is also a relationship in which teachers seemingly get the least amount of training: a trainee teacher may shadow a class teacher during parents' evening, or an ECT may be given some general guidance on what to say. But that's just learning how to communicate effectively – which is important – but how do we build a *relationship* with parents/carers.

The advice that follows is generic. A secondary teacher's relationship with parents will naturally be less developed than a primary teacher who teaches the same thirty-odd pupils every day; a secondary teacher may make more phone calls, but a primary teacher's phone calls may last longer. It really is swings and roundabouts. Take the spirit of the guidance and apply it to your individual setting.

GET OVER YOUR FEAR

For a lot of teachers, the mere possibility of an angry parent is enough to deter them from making a quick phone call home which would probably save them a lot of time (setting, then chasing up detentions, for example) and be more likely have the desired impact. You need to get over your fear.

It's not a money-back guarantee, but the overwhelming majority of parents want the same thing as teachers, i.e. the best possible outcomes for their children. In light of this, it is better (and closer to the truth!) for a teacher to view parents as people to 'work with' not 'deal with'. Also, remember that there is a considerable chance that they fear your judgement as much as you fear theirs – no one likes being on the spot! So, relax and pick up the phone. On a not-so-side note, there is far more respect for teachers from the general public than the media might lead you to believe, particularly post-Covid, so again, try not to assume the worst. The parent/carer will very much appreciate your phone call because, as well as showing that you care, you are showing personality irrespective of the reason for your call.

MAKE A POSITIVE PHONE CALL HOME

Contacting parents often comes with a negative connotation. When you decide you're going to phone home or tell a child you're going to, you can bet your new set of glue sticks that you're doing it at as a punishment or threat.

Of course, there is nothing inherently wrong with that, but the teacher–parent relationship – and therefore pupil outcomes – are greatly improved if we contact parents for positive reasons too. Naturally, the teacher–pupil relationship also improves. Why not phone home for a child who did well in the assessment, or who's always on time and displays immaculate behaviour? Don't wait until parents' evening to gushingly praise your pupils – pick up the phone.

A positive phone call home is particularly effective when it follows a sanction. For example, let's say you had to give Joe Bloggs a detention for persistent disruption and his behaviour since has shown consistent improvement. If you involved Joe's parents/carers during the poor behaviour stage, you can be sure they'd love to hear how well Joe's doing now and they'd hold you in even higher regard for telling them. Not only will your relationship improve, but Joe's behaviour is less likely to slip again.

HONESTY

It is important that you don't just tell parents/carers what (you think) they want to hear. Even a defensive parent wants honesty. This can be difficult, particularly when giving bad or otherwise not-so-positive news. To avoid the awkwardness that inevitably accompanies this, give parents/carers what is commonly dubbed the 'sh*t sandwich.' Tell them something positive, then give them the bad news, then end with something positive. So, for example, let's say you decided to phone home after giving Joe Bloggs two consecutive detentions for constantly talking out of turn. Say something to the effect of: 'Jo can be very interested in science when he wants to be, and he has so much potential. Unfortunately, I've had to give him another detention this week because he just keeps talking while I'm trying to teach – constantly distracting others and disrupting their learning. Hopefully we can give him the support he needs to get his behaviour back on track and be the good lad we know he can be.' The sh*t sandwich is much easier for you to serve and far easier for the parent to eat (sorry!). You're more likely to get the parent/carer onside and the teacher–parent relationship remains intact.

HINTS AND TIPS

If a parent/carer doesn't answer the phone it is worth leaving a message, in which case, consider the following format when reporting something negative:

- Introduce yourself, e.g. Hi. This is Mr Akbar. I'm the science teacher of Joe Bloggs.

- Begin with a positive, e.g. Joe shows a lot of enthusiasm in xyz.

- Then state the negative behaviour/action: e.g. unfortunately, he's been late to science twice this week.

- Ask them for support: e.g. I'd kindly appreciate your support in getting his punctuality back on track.

- Thank them.

Of course, it is much easier when phoning for a positive reason!

KNOW THE CHILD BEFORE CONTACTING PARENTS/CARERS

Imagine you rang Joe's parents/carers to inform them of his recent disruptive behaviour only to be met with – 'Were you not aware of his recent ADHD diagnosis?' or 'He's having a difficult time at the moment as I've just been diagnosed with cancer.' To avoid embarrassment and doing serious damage to the teacher–parent relationship, make sure you are familiar with the individual needs, life situation, etc. of the child of any parent/carer you decide to contact. You will likely know most things anyway, but have a quick look on the system just to make sure in case something's been added or amended. If possible, it's also worth asking pastoral leads or even another teacher if they've spoken to the said parent/carer before and, if so, what are they 'like'? The more you know the better you can prepare for the discussion as well as show your expertise. The teacher–parent relationship will improve and consequently, so will pupil outcomes.

ANGRY PARENT?

While you have nothing to fear the overwhelming majority of the time, it is still worth noting that if you do come across an angry parent, you can be as certain as you are about being put on cover during your PPA time that it's not *you* the parent is angry at. (When angry at a teacher, rarely does a parent approach them directly, rather, they'll phone the school and rant to a school leader). More often than not, it will be some communication failure that's bothered them and that will likely involve more than just the classroom teacher (see the next section for how to avoid this). For now, the general rule for dealing with an angry parent is to allow them to speak, try not to get defensive and reassure them that you will take on their concerns. And, of course, if you get unlucky and it *is* personal and they start being rude, abusive or aggressive, hang up or walk away and report them afterwards.

 ## REFLECTION POINTS

What preconceived notions do you think some parents/carers may have that can inhibit the teacher–parent relationship? How do you think you can overcome these barriers?

BE QUICK WHEN SHARING INFORMATION

Nothing bothers a conscientious parent more than finding out too late: Joe's been misbehaving in maths; the teacher doesn't tell mum and dad until parents' evening. Kareem's underperforming in science; his parents only find out when they see red on his data report. Michelle got the highest mark in the last five French tests; her grandmother had no clue.

In order to keep the teacher–parent relationship intact, share information with parents at the earliest opportunity whenever possible. If you are unaware of what should be shared, ask yourself – *would I say this on parents' evening*? If so, then share it earlier. Of course, there aren't enough hours in the day for you to do this for every single pupil in your care, so for the sake of your workload, inform parents/carers when you start to see *patterns emerging*: phone Joe's parents after the second detention. Phone Michelle's grandmother after the second assessment. Phone Kareem's parents when you can see he's consistently not making any effort. Parents/carers will appreciate your proactivity and pupil outcomes are more likely to improve.

SHARE YOUR STRATEGIES

Parents/carers appreciate teachers more when they know exactly what we do for their child to maximise their potential. You don't have to give them an earful of teaching jargon but do share your strategies where it seems fitting. For example, with almost all GCSE exams being entirely at the end of year 11, a secondary school teacher has to encourage their pupils to revise throughout years 10 *and* 11 and not just save revising for the few weeks before the GCSEs. It is a good idea for the teacher to tell the parents how they're aiding revision, for example by recapping prior knowledge at the beginning of every lesson. Another example: Let's say on parents' evening you meet the mother of a child with ADHD. Feel free to casually slip in there that you limit the child's distractions by sitting them away from their friends, you give short, concise instructions, chunked tasks, etc. When parents/carers know the details, they acknowledge our hard work and naturally the teacher–parent relationship strengthens.

BE AVAILABLE

Depending on the age range you teach, you may be able to consider building some 'surgery time' into your working week during which parents have the opportunity to liaise with you (and you them) in a less formal setting.

Simply informing parents that you're in your classroom and free to chat until 4pm on a Tuesday, for example, would do wonders for the teacher–parent relationship. If time doesn't allow that, make yourself available by being present at the school gates at the end of the day, once or twice a week, and 'catch-up' with parents if/when necessary.

RESPOND IMMEDIATELY

No one (in UK schools at least!) is expecting you to stop teaching and action an email from an angry parent, claiming their daughter Chloe has lost her PE kit. It isn't in the last place she looked, they say, so they'd like you to try and find it. (Because you've got so much time on your hands and want to get your daily steps in, of course.)

Jokes(?) aside, while it is rarely the case that a teacher is expected to action a parent's request immediately, it *is* a good idea to *respond* immediately. In the above example, the teacher should reply with a simple. *Thank you. I will get back to you by [insert day/time].* In this way, you maintain a good relationship with the parent by validating their concerns, but you don't do so at cost of your own wellbeing.

BE MINDFUL OF TIME

You will come across the odd parent who will bend your ear back for 20 minutes straight, repeatedly making the same point over and over again. If that happens and you don't have the time to deal with it, simply say: 'The caretaker is about to lock up, I have to go.' Then say bye and hang up. The teacher–parent relationship is important but so is your wellbeing.

FURTHER READING

For more tips on how to engage parents/carers, check out A Little Guide for Teachers – Engaging Parents and Carers by Emma Kell and Clemmie Stewart.

NOTE IT DOWN

FREQUENT POSITIVE COMMUNICATION IMPROVES THE TEACHER-PARENT RELATIONSHIP. EVERY HALF-TERM, MAKE A POSITIVE PHONE CALL TO THE PARENTS/CARERS OF FIVE PUPILS WHO ARE LESS ENGAGED WITH SCHOOL THAN THEIR CLASSMATES (COMMONLY INDICATED BY LOW ATTENDANCE AND ACHIEVEMENT). MAKE NOTES IN THE TABLE BELOW SO YOU CAN HAVE SOME IDEA OF THE IMPACT OVER TIME.

HALF-TERM 1:

Pupil	Reason for Call

HALF-TERM 2:

Pupil	Reason for Call

HALF-TERM 3:

Pupil	Reason for Call

CONCLUSION

Thriving teachers build relationships in subtle and not-so-subtle ways, consciously and unconsciously employing very specific techniques.

A teacher's success in this area is often perceived to be a product of some elusive quality possessed by the individual. Granted, this is not without some merit as not everything is quantifiable and explaining why some teachers are just better at it than others is not always easy. Nonetheless, you can see that there is a lot we can do (and not do!) to build positive relationships at school and we should maximise on this.

As you progress through your career, make it a habit to regularly evaluate your relationships in the six strands. Go back to each chapter and give yourself some unwritten relationship targets each academic year, because how you relate to your class, to individual pupils, to fellow teachers, to school leaders, to support staff and to parents/carers will be a key determinant of your wellbeing, progression, overall job satisfaction and of course, of pupil outcomes.

Remember also that no relationship exists in isolation: your relationship with fellow teachers will impact your relationship with school leaders; your relationship with individual pupils will impact your relationship with your class, and so on. Maintain a holistic approach, accepting of course, that strengths and weaknesses are inevitable, and this is ok.

While relationships can have a profound impact, they are not a silver bullet, and a perceived lack thereof must never be used as a scapegoat. If your class is misbehaving, for example, it must not automatically be assumed that it's due to your lack of effort in building a relationship. If a parent refuses to engage with you, no guilt on your part should be assumed.

We only have control over – surprisingly enough – the things we have control over.

We can't do everything, but we can do a lot!

INDEX